# WATERFALLS

Also by Maggie O'Sullivan

In the House of the Shaman (1993)
red shifts (2001)
Palace of Reptiles (2003)
"all origins are lonely" (2003)
Body of Work (2006)
Windows Opening (2007)
ALTO (2009)
murmur (2011)

*(with Bruce Andrews)*
eXcLa (1993)

*As editor:*
Out of Everywhere: linguistically innovative poetry
by women in North America and the UK (1996)

*Audio:*
her/story:eye (CD, 2004)
States of Emergency (CD, 2005)

*About Maggie O'Sullivan:*
The Salt Companion to Maggie O'Sullivan (2011)

# WATERFALLS

# Maggie O'Sullivan

REALITY STREET

Published by
REALITY STREET
63 All Saints Street, Hastings, East Sussex TN34 3BN, UK
www.realitystreet.co.uk

Second (paperback) edition 2012
First published in a limited edition by etruscan books, 2009

Back cover photo by Charles Bernstein
Original typesetting by Robert W Palmer, Tuff Talk Press, Uley, Gloucestershire

A catalogue record for this book is available from the British Library

ISBN: 978-1-874400-57-8

*Acknowledgements*
These works that are *Waterfalls* have appeared in the following journals and
anthologies – thanks to the editors and publishers involved: *AND* no 9;
*Conductors of Chaos*; *Etruscan Jetty – Anthology of the 6 Towns Poetry Festival*; *RWC*
no 35; *etruscan reader III – Maggie O'Sullivan, David Gascoyne, Barry MacSweeney*;
*Pages* 421-445; *ON WORD (Part One) – An anthology of contemporary poetry and
method*.

*winter ceremony* was a 6 Towns Poetry Festival commission – "For the Locker and
the Steerer" 1996.

To Daniel, my father
(26th January 1917 – 9th June 2004)

your heart, your songs

## pre-text

a house far-opens   who, what – sudden breathed, Sky  Sky

considering belongs – budding traces – getting method determined,

the seemed subject wrote; sure, the whole unmixed glancing riotous

threads & disadvantage it.  make a course less  in-in in-is dimensions

- worn – down, broke –


now even addressing the out-memory, shadows keen more candidly.

WELL I NURSED &

    CARRIED

        THEIR LIGHT TO

            BRIMMING

                AVID BUD –

                    SHEER & TOUCHING

                      TO LEAF –

                        STARK

                        FURZE

                            PURPLER TO CROW –

                                SOFT RAN

                        LITTERS OF I –

              ---      A BIT SINCE DID I

            EAT ---

            ´TWAS ALL ALONG

           VINEGAR LILT

        OF THE HILLS´

       UNWISE ARIAS

     WASHING

    INSIDE MY RIBS –

   INJUST –

 UN-

OF A LARGER TERRAIN

SWERVISH –

                              DWINDLED
                        BODES THE SHIFT –
                      ALL SICKLY JUTTINGS
                    OF ME –
                  FRAIL CRAFT
                AFLOAT ON
              SKULL –
            TUMBLED
          NETTLE´S
        SULLEN FROTH –
      UNTYING LIPS
    TO MAGPIE´S BULGED FLYING –
  DONE-UP
UN-
    COLOUR-
      UN-

        JAW/TONGUE´S
        WEEP-WEEP
          PROCEDURES –

              ONE BY ONE
                I´VE LET THEM
                        MUTTER ME
                    AWFUL SLOW
                          WITHERING –

NO –

    NOT ONE –

        ANSWERS THEIR NAME –

                              DICE OVERTY

                        ENTURTLED TURTLEY

                                  AFFERY

                                      ALLA

                        PLUCKILY BROKE –

                      p p p p p p p p p p p  pur –

                            PLUCKED – PLUCKED –

                      PUCKERINGS –

                p p p p p p p –

                PUT TO –

             I

          DUSK UTTER FEWS

        WHITE FEWER

      MY LIPS

       A

     BOUNDING

   FEATHER

  STIFFENED

DEPLORABLY –

  NOW

                        THEN

                HERE

            THERE –


        – WHAT´S MORE
      A BIT SINCE DID I –
SO SUDDENED –
    SO TILT –
        NO –
            CYGNET PEARLY TIPTIC
            FLAUNT & WOKE --


                A BIT SINCE DID I ----


                I DOWNRIGHT
                TWIG –
                    PEEPED /


                    PUTTERED / LOLLING
                SHUT´S WAY –

UNLEVEL UN-
STITCHING
IS --


CREPT –
AVER –
avert –
unseen –
teeming / impeded /
pale hung
HEMMED /
SPARE –
KEPT BOAT
KEEN UPON ITS LONGING –


AIR-STRUCK –


DANGLED –


SHEEREST –


IT´S MY SHADOW NOW – .
BROODING PEBBLE
ON A THREAD –
THE BOILED BLOODY
DRIZZLE –
VOWELLING
NOTHIN´ ATALL

                        THAT ROOFS
                    THE PALPITANT SHIMMER –
            HERE –


                WHERE I WAITED  /  WAITED
            FOR THEM –
        PLURALS OF HORSE –
        BAREFOOT –
    BOYS
    ARRIVEDLY –

MANYS THE BLUSH
WHINNIED CULOUSLY DOES –
(THE HEART –
        red-still-of-a-did –
            THE LINE OF THE RED
                crush of i
                    bled –
                    TO THE UN-
                        WANT &
                            DIMMED INCLINE
                            NETTED  / n –
                            NOTCHINGS
                            HOOVED TO –
                                GAUNT STENCH  /  THE UNFIT  /
                                STILLY DUG
                                STINKING SKIN OF ME –
                                    s t u t t e r i n g  ----

SO CONSTRAINED A SKY
              PERSISTS
              QUICKEST
       CONSONANCE OF PURPLE --
                   TENSED
                   AS IF
              UNCOPPERING
                   SOURS
                    OF EAR
                    & LIMB
                 IN A DITCH –

                    THE WOMB –
                    what womb?
                      FROM ITS HUE –
                         HURTLES --
                   detached –
                 TREMBLEY –

               JUXTA-STREWN  /
             BLACKENED  /

       ROAMS

      THE HAIR SO –
      BLEW OUT
     SOOT OF ME –
     – SNOW SYLLABLE
    THUDS –

– AJAR –

                              rope round the legs –
                          broken glass in the socket –
                        GLASS IN THE SKY –
                      JUGILY JUGILY RINGS
                    PANGS / PA /
                  STEERAGED
              BRIAR, EYE --
          SUNK
        GAPING –
    LONGED –

PULLING IN / SWINGING
    THE SCREECH –
        – HITTING IT –


        – A FIST you'd --------


        AFOOT


        LOPSIDED –


        SO –

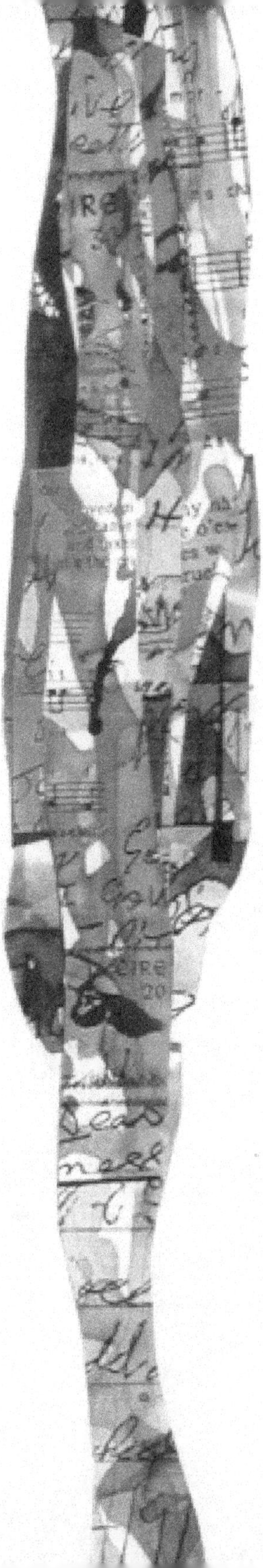

**– that bread should be –**

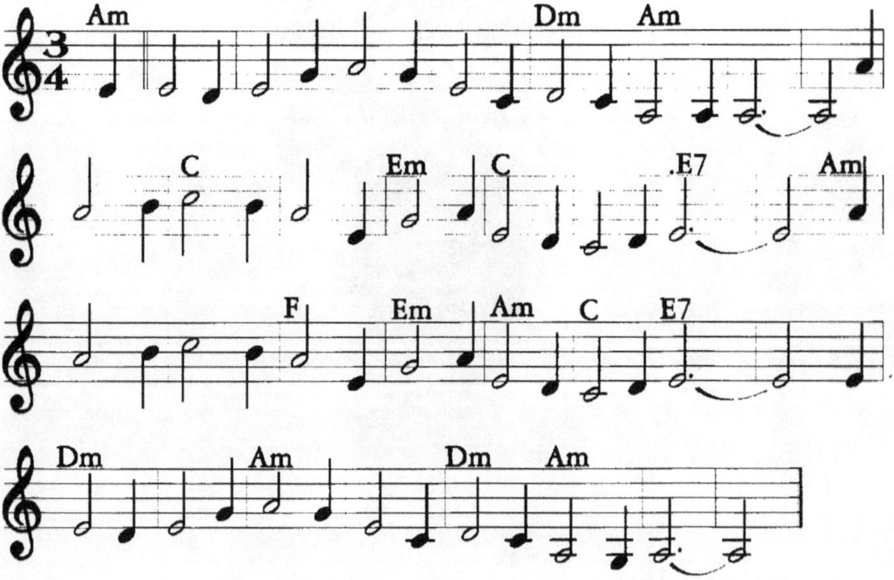

AN SCIOBAIRIN

SCIO BREIDHE

SCIOBADH AR DHION

SCIOBADH

UISCE BREAN

low ground long black crêpe rolled in the mouth's threshing

gleam & misty blood dripping so many red threads

the maps are become

(how'd soak) –


what hacked what shatters –


round round as an O's hoop scouring vowels –

my hand       /

                    his

                          /

          rounds, Rosary      /

                                B

                                    u

                                       c

                                          k

                                             l

                                                e

                                                   d

          SAYING / DECADES

                    Shone Blue

<u>going up to the small handy little farm the father's house</u>

every stone every  S /

t

u

m

b

l

e

d

BLED ———

run – through –
consonant of hearth –
dead twigs air UNEVEN –

Armfuls ————————

   left

        /

               standing

      <u>ASH</u>

         /

              <u>it is of an age with the house</u>

             – its

Knee-Deep unbrokenSINGING its Acred Heart's
Umbilicus Chirruping
that Shielding Ash of memory bleeding
Sea-Saw fearments
Eared –
Eyed –
(Bough Siblings of No Fixed SONG/

S

  c

    a

     t

      t

       e

        r

         e

          d

anywhere    but    I    –

       half–starved–half–clothed–half–eaten–by ————

              half–any–speech   ————

              half–any

       rip in the sky's Blue mantling rag for an O ————

           dragged

       out of their stares

    their own filthy rots hanging

screamsticks –    white skull over bone  –

       )sewing it over  –

   LAPWINGS TAKE MY COLD PIPING  ————————

ill –

ailed iller ill -ill -illeDDDDDDDDD –

shrap & feral toolings –

SINGS –


why scarlet?          uncoiling

was it sea rail of skull's red dicing

entrail here entrails asks-she-in of axe ————

WHERE FOR THE AXE IF I'VE ——————————

       UNSINGING NOT,

             SOUND NO ——————————

                    Neither go    /    going about of a story or

shows that i – i'd to do – i ——————

Neither Assimilated nor –

       middle of No – (tunes keeping

       me –

           unsteady –

                 Blood leaks

                        rackety plume never heard ———

Seeing eye of the story counts          yet it is

    tilted, rigged, dragging at the haemorrhage of uns –

my body, (sever, sever who shall she see?

                              skulls

                       keened out in the rain

         && back on the wind would come the tottering twist

    (stank, stank bone jointed                re-twining

its own circle

        what way a horse can fall?

            t   h   i   s

     m

        a

        n

          y

<u>the fitness of names</u> –      spittle in a crock

    re-carving the Spells

   so manys red loud ear    red hooves    ruby live beaten

    thing soft red south so –


               my belly my throat –

    sick sundering heap   – a crimson talking backwards

      gripping fora
            way against the abscessed cotted struggling

          with sun pulled up ––––––––

few scrapes of the shovel ————

    searching in our soils   /   the lot of long silent letters /

       searching   /   searching ——


        peeling it off the rended spine   ————

S

   E

     V

       E

         R

           E

             D

        laid bare the narrative i SINGING

W I R E     nettle

in the mouth

unevenly & acute

the jagged narrow –

the jagged narrow vertical roofed over with sticks and wild cresses ⸻

drawing stones all day on a few ribs to the moon

my guts trail out my eyes & the mucks're

thronging wet ——————

MAGPIE'S

black feet slap their brink on the

stems not a ground i tread –

cavity-sippling –

the <u>blight</u> the distemper the————

whole families without a trace my ————————

                                       dealt ———

     it occurs:        ————————

the unstory

     –   that bread should be  –

Song's bleeding wove

       (never more crow – scraping

CENTURIES      ACENTURY'S

hard plain howl –

their kids Leaping

the house

A

S

K

A

N

C

E

– Stalkic Chieftain's Bird –


that's how we


S   P   E   L   L   E   D   )

back in I ————————

Beast Moan brooched Breath's cold straw little boats

Many a one

o-u-t

on the hills' inexact shimmer

there shoulder & drank

drove air

raven     ravening
Ravenous

R A V I N E —————

remnants –

Hare going up

down

Buds gone so ) –

rocks to us ———

—————————————

# <u>winter ceremony</u>

caoi chadhan in oidhche fhuair
(or geese grieving in the cold night)

from *Ní Binn Do Thorann Lem Thaoibh*
  (*Ugly Your Uproar at My Side*)

  – anonymous 17th century Irish poem

down of moon

deeply

1`long


H A R E S

going so

flew/
                    nt –


QU
(about eight or ten letter i cant pronounce

s t r e t c h i n g

g o n e - o n - t o  _____

– sedulous

– what d ) –

dandelion
earths
&
all
rising humming over
the season we weep in

'S

'S

'S,

or the letters  s, u, n - (some double the s) S's of
the word – the word SUN – SUN sheer spurted

 all seeing – sees –
COLTSFOOT
Yellow Hoopness –

lovely bit of sun ————————————
                    sun
                    sun
                    SUILE
                    SUILE
                    SUILE


               shone out –
                        ‖




Did you see tumbled silent studs of crow
hovering Ox Red Alder Lake of small birds
                    her face's
                black feather?
                        ‖

She had 7 sons.  It begins with her by the door
there to the mountains.  They left from here –
all their births lain to her as I   – Bundlemost
Infant   –  as I  –  curled in the trickling scald
they moved upon –

> Once –
>
> An' Once –
>
> Once upon –
>
> Once Upon Thorn Hill
>
> Thorn Hill
>
> in the townland of Curragh
>
> off the Marsh Road
>
> out of Skibbereen
>
> in the much invaded & ancient
>
> province of Munster,
>
> province of Áine,
>
> Áine – pre-Celtic
>
> Sun-Goddess
>
> Áine of the Banside,

Áine of Music &

Harp & Song &

Poetry –

Once Upon –

there was a woman once living

tall in her long black cloak

& sootblack bonnet was the way

she used to go

carrying the lantern

over

    feathers

      feather dipping feet

       feast a few fit

        little dances

         she did –

          she did –

once the father was going up to the quarry –

over six foot –

the pool –

where he'd quarried the blue stone for the house

and she shivering we all dead – was gone in –

couldn't put it out of her –

that doing away –

not once but many times –

and only for he pulling her back –

she'd be –

i heard the geese pleat lake white feather drools
of oval twist & sudden abject tenure

                                    i'd seen

the grainey ones shuffling on in the broken dragging
rain shuttered steep

                              without

mourning (or ceremony)  burying on

                & in the sky

<u>my father reaping the corn – my mother behind –</u>

<u>piling 'n binding</u>

             spelling

i huge Black & White Magpie –

              Magpie heartgown –

              Magpie heartwork –

              Magpie Heartrise – Rise – Faoi do chois!


        RISE


            WORDS


                 of


                    EVERY

nearly all dead or broken the small flock purpling to
splattered pennanular shreds as i unpeeled them from
the wire they had stuttered into –

 

                                            & as i brought
water & hummed them back into themselves with all
my heart each-bird-bird-each-body began to stir from
its shine-leaned ruin its festering tattered cage into
its flighting dwell – its gooseness

## WHAT • ASH • TREE

she'd be –

drowned –


ing-Be great CROUCH cú cú peeps

watering pitchBla Blackened fu

furlful sack-torrent's

bending drizzle - - -


mouth of dog ---

child's head

i set over --- hadn't it ---


---

IMPEARLS TO FEATHER

feathering & stars


stagg-e-r-r-i-n-g

at rest    CONVULSE - - -

the bloodless

failing


lit   lit   lit


FINGERS IN BEHIND EYE—

GAPE EARLIER

FUNERARY DRIVING

SKY WHITE RUSHES


BLUE


s-P-O-O-L-I-N-G


BELLOW

BROWED RISING LIP RINSED PLAINS

I ROCKED

& fell to leafing

THE CROSSING OF RUSHES & MORE BLOOD

BLED UNTIL IT WAS HER

word words

stroked

on a branch


heartbeat's –

(countering – – – – – – –

encountering

kind of – – – – – – –

singing – – – – – – –


BARE like BASKET from BATTLE

BEGINISH –

===============

...Is that the speech of her her

        ropes hutted a still

               rioted clawning leaf

  ...Is that the heart of her her


       lifting   lifting

  ...as in azure's conching sprint –


ASSEMBLEFUL.&.DIFFER/

BLESS-TINT TINGING FLOOD MADE HIGH I

    DROWNED A PAPER BUTTERFLY INSIDE ME

  DEAD SWIRL OF STICKS THE RAVENS LET FALL

          PELTING


       clip   clip   clip



    THEHOOVES –


DID YOU KNOW THE AIR – THE WASH OF HAZEL

      MAPPED ON THE SWING OF HER SIGHT?


    ------------

I USED SEE MY MOTHER
    CLAWING UP THE SIDES OF THE LAND –
    HERON BURDOCKS
    HER EMBRACES
    & FEVERS

        ARCHED 0 – FLOODED 0 –
0 – STONES –
OVERT & SEVERE –
loop of Error –
Splitting the Ear's
    bright sobbing


    frayed


    puckered


    incurable

rotting &


i – d – i – o – t

with lock
  & webbed fork
    brownfriezegreylinen   TANDEM SHAWLIE
      SHAWL RAVENS


        PEBBLEST
OF SKELETON


SUCH AS I –
WHAT WAS THROWN ALIVE ON A SLOPE


   EYELID OF SORTS –
      k i n  – i n  – i n –
    d l i n g  –
  l – N – G  – HAWKED ─────────

WHEN HEN IN ALL
STAMMER'S FAIR SEEP
& FIX & EVERY
TIARA LIGHT'N TUG OF THE AIR
OVER & O –
KEENED
OUT OF SEA –
SON –

ohs –

O mouth

O –

o –

scattering quenched fire/hearth/heart/into

water


she cursed
& sank bird-headed birds were to settle & fasten
them the last white ashes round her neck

salving of the sticks

laters, is dead

new, afloat




WHOSE OWN CORPSE  .

WHOSE WOULD CARRY IT  .   ashingly cloa & skull   .

WHOSE OWN SHOULDERING RAIN = RAN as in

Accordian Birthing  .  WHOSE OWN GAUNTING

SONG – BETTER-BE-VULGING  .  PLUCKED  .  PLUCKED

AS FAR AS COULD  .   so nearly swu - severed - cant

swi – WHOSE WOULD BLUNT REJOICE  .  WHO LIPS THE

SPREADING FINGERS at its high f e a s t i n g

throat  .   WHOSE OWN STORY HOWLS & SOBS THE

BLEEDED LIMBICS ASUNDER  .   WHOSE OWN STORY SHOOK

THE PLURALS  .  SHOOK THE DENTS  .  SHOOK  .

SHOOK THE BRINKS IN BLUNDER  .

showering

        bare earth

        unmarked


    purpling dead

      stumbling over, stumbling over

         ||

      the father used give the stone a wash

        so it shone from the hill –

        white for miles around –

         ||

         walls thick as ever –

        the roof – the door

        gone after them –

         ||

great Sweep of Magpie –

Young Magpies'

time now –


i counting to the life


asking after, asking after

i'd say animal

———————————————— putting spirit ————————————

nor is the moon

extinguished

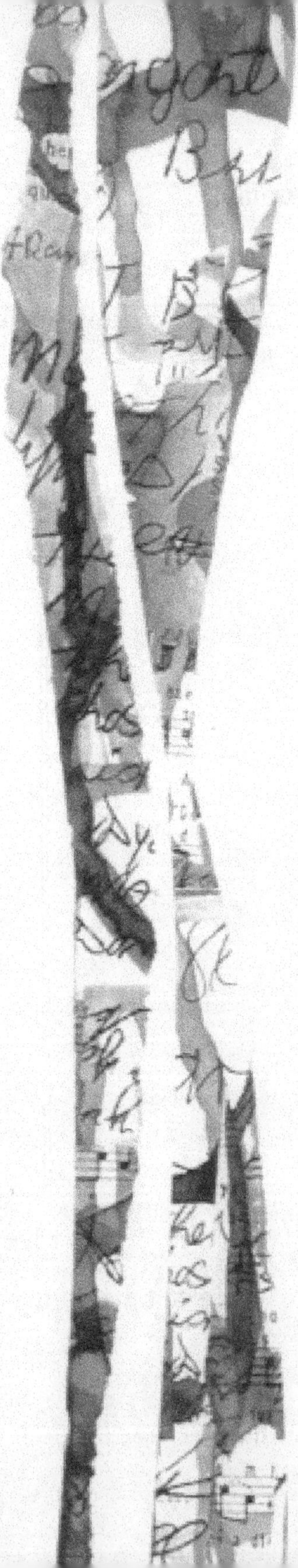

## own land

If.Of.Off

/

Off.Chance.Birth.**BEING**.  (Bing.Bing.**BLACK**,
as.**BLACKBIRD**.in.spring) –

Dandelion prongs d'd  d'down  ownded,  shin

did so ———

Coatsleeves, Pebble ——

   Lopely Fetches – Peeps – Trembling ——

      nor skein of all reek

         Nor heal nor air of snarls

      Nor next nor near-doubly sped & rotting

Nor sub HUE   Nor saddle, nor housings


   countenance her tossing,

<u>nor so</u> ——

<u>is.was.so</u>

knawvshawling torrents

littlest              stared into          ever so little

less as flies          word for **Thrived,**          **Leapt**

– (it was hers

jumped the ravine) –

driven crimson

Skiffs —

hearses

(re)

hearses

Leaps into B –

Bee–Up

all of a Baa          Bake down banks

Bockety        Brags        Blighted marred spoiled,
                                    happened, said –

                    bright
            Bronzy shonner
                slants –

        Own Beast puckered moons –

        Lopped –

appal –

        Poet –

who'd be?)  – of.it.you – Weaver of Spells, <u>EARER</u> –
hey-go-merry-go-higgledy Hurling

REMEMBRANCER – (herited . here/it'd . here it is .
heretic . heresies . here she is . here her is . in
her it .  ) –

<u>Inheritances</u>

<u>In Here She Dances</u>

crabbit

crawsick                    cawhake

chaw

dwinderings - daubings, d'dent —

down around didn't her up   every one in a . ) –

combing & songing & combing

the fretty pestered shunts ————————

# WATERFALLS

DHUINE LE DIA / DIAlogue

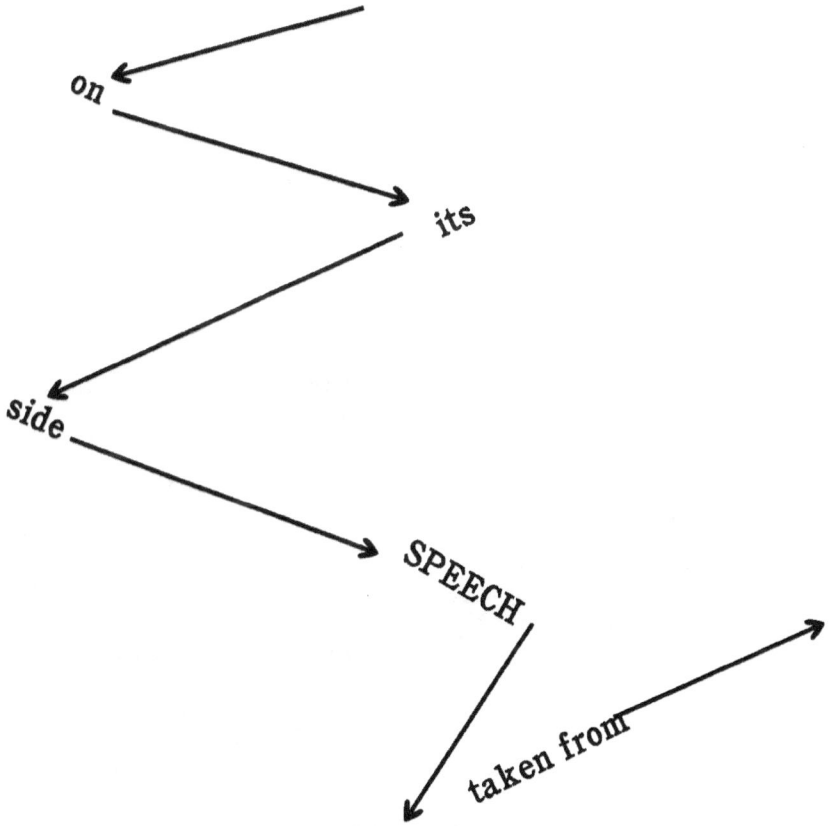

on

its

side

SPEECH

taken from

THIS HOUSE
constantly
THIS HOUSE

an eye gone out along, an eye from the hare's

hue jest
wildered slant scrawed eartish
looping medal & holy
Eye'uv
eye'ity
Eye'uv
SKULL in her lap-most
Bit & Chant
of Sobs ———

do

bleed

&

drip

&

drench & ———

gouge

– nothing to ocean the lips –
– but root's eroded acume –
– intuppancy shoved –
on the moon's
lastingness and passing ———

(as a whisper) ———

(as a whisper)          EYED AS A WHISPER

                        YES

                        THE SHEER

                        RAW

                          GOING HUNGRY ————

                         USED WAIL

                        OUR SLAUGHTERED BREATH  ————

                        COULD ONLY WHISPER

                        (YELLED IT ALL OUT  –

                        PALE SKELETAL ABODE–

                        s-REPAIR

                        & WITH ITS

                        RAZORING CAME

                        THAT COLD LEANING/

                        BLEEDING

                        WATER –

                        FALLING–


                        (ONCE THOUGH SHE –

                        RISING–

NO – MOVE –

i said animals

SHUDDERED UP TO THE thump thump thump

numb castles    spancelled wil willow

accoustic locutionsdrizzled

       WHY'D PLURALS  –

       LEAPING THEM  –

SELVES

SO OFTEN BATTERED – SO TORSO

GAPPED SO –

sew'in'it,

reaving

      rearing


     ribbons

    t / tink (of her

dipthong sundering

con,


        dimmed

## Are You Feathers?

multiple and endless

pitch, smeared shoulderways raven – took it from / took it back – Can you

make out that now?

the roped air i side with —


years'd —
notion of a step numb &
shaky gown    Seclusioning Twilight    WON'T BOW
THE KNEE    WON'T SCRAPE THE GROUND    So it was –
Grief of the Keen's
tumulary plucking threshold
herled
whoved
so –


veer /
teeing

ribs quick shadowing

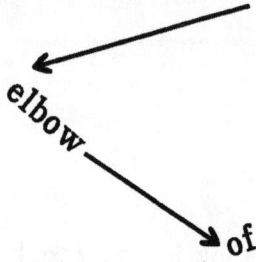

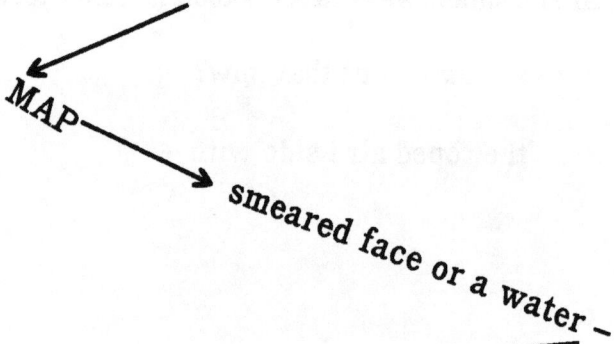

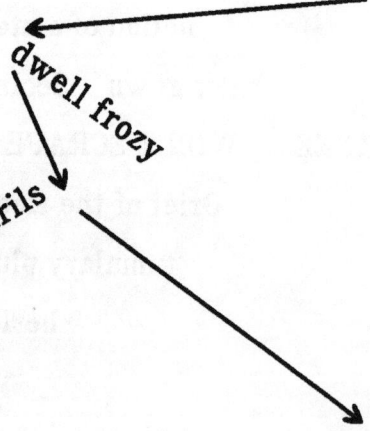

elbow

of

MAP

smeared face or a water –

dwell frozy

rag or two tendrils

stickpenny glitter

stems  in the day Seventh of May Lapwing See from Other

fasting on the doorstep

at whose door    snowly that of chant
as-she-EARS-as-she-ENTERS

## the Seventh page

•

•

•

the Pauses are as vital

~~Sun tattoo~~

~~womb's leaf~~ ~~supping~~

•

•

•

Notes:

**– that bread should be –**
**that bread should be so dear and human flesh so cheap** was the oft
repeated cry during the Irish Famine of 1845-52. The opening music
is from *Old Skibbereen*, the ballad associated with the Famine and the
Irish diaspora. My paternal family are from outside
Skibbereen, West Cork.


winter ceremony
**Ni Binn Do Thorann Lem Thaoibh** (Ugly Your Uproar at My Side) is
from *An Duanaire 1600-1900, Poems of the Dispossessed*, ed. Sean
O Tuama, trans: Thomas Kinsella, (Republic of Ireland: Dolmen, 1994).

# Selected REALITY STREET titles in print

## Poetry series
Maggie O'Sullivan (ed.): *Out of Everywhere* (1996)
Denise Riley: *Selected Poems* (2000)
Ken Edwards: *eight + six* (2003)
Redell Olsen: *Secure Portable Space* (2004)
Peter Riley: *Excavations* (2004)
Allen Fisher: *Place* (2005)
Tony Baker: *In Transit* (2005)
Jeff Hilson: *stretchers* (2006)
Maurice Scully: *Sonata* (2006)
Maggie O'Sullivan: *Body of Work* (2006)
Sarah Riggs: *chain of minuscule decisions in the form of a feeling* (2007)
Carol Watts: *Wrack* (2007)
Jeff Hilson (ed.): *The Reality Street Book of Sonnets* (2008)
Peter Jaeger: *Rapid Eye Movement* (2009)
Wendy Mulford: *The Land Between* (2009)
Allan K Horwitz/Ken Edwards (ed.): *Botsotso* (2009)
Bill Griffiths: *Collected Earlier Poems* (2010)
Fanny Howe: *Emergence* (2010)
Jim Goar: *Seoul Bus Poems* (2010)
Carol Watts: *Occasionals* (2011)
James Davies: *Plants* (2011)
Paul Brown: *A Cabin in the Mountains* (2012)

## Narrative series
Ken Edwards: *Futures* (1998, reprinted 2010)
John Hall: *Apricot Pages* (2005)
David Miller: *The Dorothy and Benno Stories* (2005)
Douglas Oliver: *Whisper 'Louise'* (2005)
Ken Edwards: *Nostalgia for Unknown Cities* (2007)
Paul Griffiths: *let me tell you* (2008)
John Gilmore: *Head of a Man* (2011)
Richard Makin: *Dwelling* (2011)
Leopold Haas: *The Raft* (2011)
Johan de Wit: *Gero Nimo* (2011)

*Go to www.realitystreet.co.uk, email info@realitystreet.co.uk or write to the address on the reverse of the title page for updates.*

REALITY STREET depends for its continuing existence on the Reality Street Supporters scheme. For details of how to become a Reality Street Supporter, or to be put on the mailing list for news of forthcoming publications, write to the address on the reverse of the title page, or email **info@realitystreet.co.uk**

Visit our website at: **www.realitystreet.co.uk**

## Reality Street Supporters who have sponsored this book:

David Annwn
Tina Bass
Andrew Brewerton
Peter Brown
Clive Bush
John Cayley
Adrian Clarke
Dane Cobain
Mary Coghill
Ian Davidson
David Dowker
Derek Eales
Carrie Etter
Michael Finnissy
Allen Fisher
Sarah Gall
John Gilmore
Giles Goodland
Paul Griffiths
Charles Hadfield
Catherine Hales
John Hall
Alan Halsey
Robert Hampson
Colin Herd
Fanny Howe
Peter Hughes
Romana Huk

Elizabeth James &
Harry Gilonis
Keith Jebb
L Kiew
Peter Larkin
Sang-Yeon Lee & Jim Goar
Richard Leigh
Tony Lopez
Chris Lord
Ian McMillan
Michael Mann
Peter Manson
Geraldine Monk
Camilla Nelson
Marjorie Perloff
Pete & Lyn
Tom Quale
Josh Robinson
Lou Rowan
Will Rowe
Peterjon & Yasmin Skelt
Hazel Smith
Valerie & Geoffrey Soar
Alan Teder
Sam Ward
Susan Wheeler
John Wilkinson
Anonymous: 11

www.ingramcontent.com/pod-product-compliance
Lightning Source LLC
LaVergne TN
LVHW041308080426
835510LV00009B/902